REACHING FOR THE HEAVENS

Excerpts from the Writings of Rabbi Adin Even-Israel Steinsaltz

מגיד
MAGGID

Steinsaltz Center
Let My People Know

In loving memory of our mother
and grandmother

Tziporah (Robyn) Ferszt z"l
צפורה בת אריה הלוי פירשט ז"ל

A lover of G-d, Torah, Am Israel
and Eretz Israel

"Grace is falsehood, and beauty is
futility, a woman who fears the Lord,
she will be praised"

"שקר החן והבל היפי אשה
יראת ה' היא תתהלל"
משלי לא, ל

Reaching for the Heavens

Excerpts from the Writings of
Rabbi Adin Even-Israel Steinsaltz

Steinsaltz Center
Maggid Books

Reaching for the Heavens:
Excerpts from the Writings of
Rabbi Adin Even-Israel Steinsaltz

First English Edition: 2022

Maggid Books
A division of Koren Publishers Jerusalem Ltd.
POB8531, New Milford, CT 06676-8531, USA
& POB 4044, Jerusalem 91040, Israel
www.korenpub.com

Originally published as *LeHarim Et HaShamayim* (Hebrew)

ISBN 978-1-59264-610-4 hardcover

Reaching for the Heavens
Excerpts from the Writings of
Rabbi Adin Even-Israel Steinsaltz

Project manager
Fruma Holland

Edited by
Evyatar Rubin

Translated by
Gaya Aranoff Bernstein

Proofreading by
Dvora Rhein

Art by
Shachar Gesundheit

Steinsaltz Center
Maggid Books

"Three possessions should you prize: a field, a friend, and a book" **Rav Hai Gaon.**

With deep gratitude, we acknowledge the support of our friend,

Rabbi Dr. Yosef Wosk.

His vision has enabled us to bring this series to publication and open the field of Jewish knowledge to all. This volume is dedicated to the reader, a fellow pilgrim on the path.

About the Author

Adin Even-Israel Steinsaltz was one of the greatest rabbis and Jewish thinkers of our generation. Through his extensive scholarly output, educational initiatives, and pedagogic brilliance, he had a profound influence on the lives of millions of Jews and non-Jews worldwide.

Rabbi Steinsaltz was a biblical and talmudic scholar. He was a mystic, an innovative educator, a keen social critic, and a worldly intellectual. *Time* magazine referred to him as a "once-in-a-millennium scholar," acknowledging the breadth and scope of his understanding of his own Jewish heritage, the religions of the world, and diverse academic disciplines. He met with heads of state, religious leaders, university professors, artists, scientists, and schoolchildre - all eager to have the privilege of being in his presence, and to learn from him.

Of all his prodigious achievements, Rabbi Steinsaltz is most renowned for his monumental work on the Talmud. His translation and commentary on the entire Talmud, made this magnum opus of Jewish learning accessible to the modern reader. This effort, as well as his commentary on biblical texts, the writings of Maimonides, and other Jewish thinkers, have led to a renaissance in Jewish learning. His books on Kabbala and Hasidic thought reveal and emphasize the relevance of mystical Jewish teachings in modern-day life. "The Thirteen Petalled Rose" and "The Soul" are two examples of his books that have been translated widely and achieved international popularity.

In recognition of his scholarly and educational accomplishments, Rabbi Steinsaltz was awarded the Israel Prize - a lifetime achievement award - as well as honors from the governments of Italy, France, and the United States. He also received honorary doctorates from multiple institutions of higher learning.

Rabbi Steinsaltz saw himself, first and foremost, as a "teacher." He visited and taught at hundreds of Jewish communities, his mantra being - "Let My People Know"; he dedicated his life to the continuity of the Jewish people and its culture. In Israel, he established a chain of elementary schools, schools of higher education, and research centers. Their unifying mission has been to promote Jewish learning and knowledge.

His deep concern for the fate of the Jewish people compelled him to travel to the Soviet Union in 1989, where he succeeded, remarkably, in establishing its first yeshiva for Jewish studies ("Lemad") and teachers' seminary. This educational center turned out to be tremendously influential in renewing Jewish life and culture in the former Soviet Union.

Rabbi Steinsaltz (1937-2020) was born, lived, and died in Jerusalem. In addition to his loving family, he is succeeded by all of the people who revered him and have learned from him. Thousands of his students and followers continue to work on carrying out and expanding his life's dream. The Steinsaltz Center in Jerusalem, whose mission remains "Let My People Know," is actively continuing the cultural and spiritual revolution that Rabbi Steinsaltz initiated.

To absorb unfamiliar information, we must first set aside some of the things we already know. Without doing this, progress is impossible and we cannot learn anything. A brief period of uncertain outcome - a kind of boundless void - accompanies any transition from one phase to the next. This is a very dangerous period of time, when anything can happen. It is like entering a body of water from dry land. There is a moment when a person is no longer on stable ground, but is not yet swimming. The longer the transition lasts, the more perilous it becomes. If we become stuck in a fixed way of thinking, we cannot advance and we can never learn.

from: Creation and Change – In Word and in Deed

Contents

The collection of essays before you is a sampling from the writings of Rabbi Adin Even-Israel Steinsaltz. The editorial choices of what to include in this volume were challenging, as it was almost impossible to distill the Rabbi's expansive views on life, the world, and Judaism into a finite number of essays. We have chosen to include essays that can be seen and understood as seeds that have the potential to grow into flowers and trees. They can also be seen as little points of the light that may have the power to illuminate the lives of others.

Rabbi Steinsaltz wrote many different types of books dealing with a wide spectrum of topics and ideas. A unifying thread in all of his writings was the intent to relate, arouse, enliven, and inspire his readers to live life more fully, more meaningfully, and more honestly. He frequently quoted the Rebbe of Kotzk, who, when asked what human beings should see as the goal of their existence, answered, "Human beings were created to raise the heavens."

For Rabbi Steinsaltz, any dream a person attempts to realize, any goal a person sets for himself, is never sufficient. And yet, even the tiniest step forward, any progress made at all, is important and meaningful.

We hope that this book will serve as a kind of portal, a gateway to spiritual paths forged by the Rabbi, to roads that lead to a life of holiness and truth.

We are grateful to Evyatar Rubin who edited this book, to Shachar Gesundheit, whose luminous artwork gives the book its unique style, and to Gaya Aranoff Bernstein, who translated this volume from the Hebrew.

Our profound gratitude for all that Rabbi Steinsaltz has given and continues to give us in his writings.

May his memory be a blessing.

Reaching Higher

Reaching Higher

A person must want to be an angel, nothing less. This is not a goal that can be realized actually, but at least a person will have tried. This is how one can come somewhat closer to an exalted level, or at least begin to ascend. One has to dream big dreams, to want to climb higher and higher. And even though it is impossible to become an angel, the desire to become one remains critical. When someone is on a path of ascent, the Holy One, blessed be He, considers the desire to be an actual accomplishment, even if the goal is not reached. If one's dreams remain on the ground, that is where the person will remain, never to ascend. It is essential to truly want to reach for the sky; it is all a matter of desire.

from the essay: Breathing Life into Elul

In all aspects of serving God, one must always try to progress, always want to do more and more. As promised in the written and oral Torah, a path is cleared for those who desire to ascend. All doors are open to a person who has made a decision to try. There is no coercion to enter any of them, but it is forbidden to remain satisfied with the status quo. Satisfaction with one's attainments is a good quality only when applied to material things; when it comes to spiritual growth, man must strive endlessly to achieve more.

Our sages exhort us: "A person must ask himself: When will my deeds reach the level of those of Abraham, Isaac, and Jacob?" Why would our sages ask us to set such an impossible, unattainable goal? The answer has to do with desire. Every person should want to achieve more, should keep dreaming, and keep trying to ascend higher and higher in the service of God.

from the essay: The Soul Within Elul

It is forbidden for a person to remain stagnant. If one does not ascend continually, one is in the process of falling. The question to ask oneself is not "Have I not held my ground?" or even "Have I performed a good deed, or have I sinned?" The questions to ask are "Have I grown? Was I a better person today than I was yesterday?" If the answer is no, then I am definitely on a path of descent. In order not to regress, one must take greater, bolder steps than before. This is not an exhortation to live an unstable existence, but rather a call to establish a committed existence that is alive with progress and renewal.

from the book: Radiance of the King

When a person keeps taking on more and more to do, one worries that he may be spreading himself too thin. In day-to-day life, there are times one can feel that he has reached the outer limits of human endeavor, and that any additional effort is physically impossible. The Lubavitcher Rebbe believed that by doing more, one can change the nature of reality. In the physical world, when great pressure is applied to an object, its essential nature can be altered. A "white dwarf" is the term given to a star that is only about the size of the earth, but has a mass much greater than that of the sun. Under pressure, the physical substance of that star became something completely different from what it had been. A person also has the potential to push boundaries beyond limits and change one's essential nature.

from the book: My Rebbe

A basic difference between human beings and the rest of creation is that people can strive toward a goal; one's deeds can reflect an overarching purpose. A horse remains a horse, and not necessarily a holy one, even if someone puts tefillin on it. Man can don tefillin, do good deeds, learn Torah, and accomplish a great deal in the course of a lifetime, but still not be much different from a horse. The true difference lies in the goal, and not in the specific deed. To be uniquely human, a person must have direction and a purpose. He must make a serious decision about the path he chooses to follow in life, and make an effort to reach the goals he has set.

from the essay: Breathing Life into Elul

A person has to see himself as a kind of candle. Before he can illuminate others, before he can become a blazing torch that can ignite the entire world, he must first enlighten his own personal existence. If his flame is weak, he deserves reproach; a flickering, sputtering flame produces very poor light. The fact that a person has free time should inspire him to jump up and get things done, rather than waste it. "How can I sleep when the world is in its current state? I must burn, I must try to create light for myself and for others. I am an individual who exists as part of a larger whole." A person needs to remain aware that time is limited and that every passing moment is irretrievable.

from the essay on "Vayetze," 5776

We believe not only in the coming of the Messiah, but also in the transformation of the world. With God's help, and with a slight effort on our part, the human race will be entirely different in the Messianic era. Not all of us can do great things, but each and every one of us can work in whatever way we can to be our best selves, despite the confines and limitations of our physical bodies. The Hebrew words *adam* (human being), *adama* (earth), and *adameh* (I will imitate) all share the letters *alef-dalet-mem*. Human beings were created from earth but we must strive to reach the heavens, and to imitate the On High (*adameh l'Elyon*), to elevate our souls. Our belief in the coming of the Messiah is essentially a belief that human beings are capable of being much better.

from the essay: The New Man

Reaching Higher

I am held accountable for things I could have tried to achieve, but did not. A person must act with the broken shards of his own reality, despite his own limitations. There are things that the Holy One, blessed be He, determines - the yield of a crop in a given year, for example - but there are also things that the Holy One, blessed be He, allows us to control. A person can learn as much as he likes; there are no limits placed on one's ability to elevate one's own soul. I am encouraged to reach toward a horizon that keeps receding farther and farther into the distance.

It is written of King Jehoshaphat: "His heart expanded on God's path." From this we understand that one must set ambitious, even unreachable goals when following God's path. I can go far on a path that has been paved by those who came before me. And I can aspire to reach its unattainable end, knowing that those who come after me will continue to follow the path, paving it one brick at a time. A person should say to himself - do not crawl if you can walk and do not walk if you can run.

Human beings must keep reaching for the heavens. There are people who see their lives in a limited way, looking backward at what they have achieved. Looking forward, anything is possible; man was created to raise his sights, to reach for the sky.

from the essay: Thirteenth of Tammuz, 5764

Big Dreams

In the Garden of Eden, God posed a question to the first human being: "Where are you?" The echo of that question still reverberates in the world. It is not always noticed, and not always heard, but it remains a persistent question, in one way or another, for every human soul. When someone hears "Where are you? Where am I?" coming from within, he may not realize that it is God who is asking. These questions arise when a person is on a path of exploration, when he knows that he has been hiding and needs to be found, to be freed. They can also come up when a person does not realize that he is hiding. They can surface during a period of frustration with a life that has no direction, and they can arise when one thinks everything is in order and understood. Awareness that these questions are actually being asked has a profound effect on one's soul. If one is truly listening, and hears the questions reverberate within, and contemplates their meaning, it is also possible to hear something above and beyond, and that is, the voice of the One asking the questions. Even when a person asks of himself - "Where am I in my world?" – it is essentially the voice of God speaking to him, from within.

from the book: The Thirteen Petalled Rose

It has been said that man is part angel, part beast. But what, in essence, is the nature of a creature comprised of angel and beast, body and soul, intellect and feeling, good and evil? The only real answer to this question is that none of these qualities alone defines a human being. What makes a person into a human being is the mix. A human being is neither angel nor beast; he is both. All possible combinations and permutations of opposing characteristics exist simultaneously in man; all comprise the full reality of human existence. A person is a complex cre ture, and though the angelic part of a person is unquestionably superior, one shouldn't conclude that man's role in life is to be a total angel. Had God wanted people to be angels, He could have created additional angels. Every human being was created with a unique combination of characteristics.

It is incumbent on each of us to strive continually to elevate our souls to reach higher and higher levels; it is forbidden to remain satisfied with one's inner beast. This task is accomplished by each human being in his own particular way; it is not achieved by trying to imitate an angel.

from the essay: Human Holiness

Throughout life, one asks the same question in many forms. This question lies at the heart of a search for oneself, a search that begins with the first glimmer of consciousness and continues to the very last breath. This search varies for every human being, at every stage of life. Often the search is conducted without any intellectual understanding; sometimes the subtlest philosophical nuances of thought may be brought into play, and at other times, the question does not even rise to the level of consciousness. But a person is never free of these essential questions: Who am I? Where have I come from? Where am I going? What for? Why?

from the book: The Thirteen Petalled Rose

Every human being has a unique soul. This uniqueness is not only a result of nature and nurture, or inheritance and learning. Every soul has its own specific divine mission; the purpose of each soul is to fulfill that mission, which in turn is part of a much greater picture. It is a role that no other human being in the world can fulfill, even though others may be smarter, holier, greater, or just better. Each soul is different from the soul of anyone else, and has qualities and characteristics that are combined in a unique way. The task of serving God in this world is divided among human beings into many little parts; the role of the first human being was to "work this world and guard it." And since the beginning of time, every soul has been given its own role to perform, so that necessary repairs of this world can be made. The particular mission of a given soul cannot be fulfilled by anyone else.

from the book: The Thirteen Petalled Rose

Although it is true that human beings are not completely free to choose their souls, or the way in which their souls are revealed, all people have the potential to connect with their loftier selves. A person must strive to do the internal work necessary to reveal the higher levels of his soul, and to make them a part of active consciousness. These elevated levels exist within every human being. Every person can transcend not only his environment or level of education, but also the ways in which his soul is revealed in those settings.

from the book: The Soul

A person can spread light in this world without having done anything considered to be exceptional. This can be done in the course of daily life. This light cannot be measured, and is not necessarily cited as an accomplishment in one's obituary. But this type of activity has significance in the final evaluation of the essence of a person's life. Sarah, our matriarch, left everyone she encountered with little points of light. Each and every one of her years was counted as a year of meaningful life. Sarah's age at the time of her death is described in the Torah in this way: "The life of Sarah was one hundred years and twenty years and seven years, the years of the life of Sarah." Like Sarah, one must try to **live** every year of life to spread light.

from the essay: the Eighteenth of Elul, 5767

When a person reaches a point in life where he is able to listen to his soul, many different reactions can follow. If he reaches this point after years of disconnectedness, after a lifetime of bad deeds and deafness to his inner voice, this new awareness will not be perceived clearly. At first it may just be sensed as a weak stirring of the soul; one may even be surprised to feel that he has a soul at all. But when a person begins to listen to the voice of the soul, and to pay attention to it, it becomes more and more distinct. Sometimes feelings arise from a person's distant past, feelings that somehow retain power. With protracted listening, not only can a person realize that he actually does have a soul, but he can also begin to hear that his soul has something to say that is relevant to his current existence.

from the book: The Soul

Sometimes a tree that is large and imposing in summer looks much less impressive in autumn. Sometimes all that remains of it after the leaves have fallen is a trunk with a few bare branches. A person can also experience a kind of autumn in life, a time when everything seems to have dried up. All that one has achieved, built up, nurtured, and completed falls away, leaving him empty. When this happens, it is essential to remember that the tree must not be cut down; it will grow back, given time and the opportunity. There are many people whose progress and growth are inhibited by the thought that something inside them has died and cannot be revived. A person can become so disillusioned that he gives up on himself. Feeling "all dried up," he loses his way and falls into bad deeds. In the real world, a tree can grow back to be as beautiful as it had been before autumn.

from the book: Change and Renewal

Time

In the Jewish world, the passage of time is not seen as a one-way stream in which past, present, and future are connected in a linear, sequential fashion. Time is perceived as two interconnected movements: a forward motion on one hand, and a circular return on the other. The concept of time in Judaism can be envisioned as a spiral structure that began with creation and is in constant motion, stretching forward and turning back. We return repeatedly to a past that is never over and done. It changes as multiple cycles of return interconnect in the ever-evolving present.

Days, weeks, and years have their own cycles. There is the cycle of the hours of the day, the cycle of the week, and the cycle of the month, the cycle of the year, and writ large, the cycle of sabbaticals and jubilees. There are also great cycles of one thousand years, and of seven thousand years. No two moments in time can ever be the same.

from the book: The Thirteen Petalled Rose

The ideal Jewish way to live life is to live in the present, not to behave as if life begins in the future, nor to see youth as a mere planning stage for adulthood. Neither to spend old age being nostalgic for the past. Not to diminish the significance of the present, not to waste its preciousness. Life is not to be spent dreaming of future happiness; it is to be lived fully, now, when the joy and gift of being alive is close and real and palpable. Fulfillment, if at all possible, can be found in equal measure in each stage of life. If there is a need to repair aspects of one's life, this remains true for every stage.

from the essay: From Childhood to Old Age, Internalizing Education

The purpose of time in our lives is to live each moment, not just to spend it, or to pass it. A person can get so enmeshed in the details of life that the critical question is forgotten. A person can even feel concern about past deeds, and remorse in the month of Elul, but the main question to be answered is always – Was life actually lived? In order to be truly alive one does not have to be doing anything special. A person can be fully alive while learning a page of Gemara, or reading a chapter of Tehillim. It is also possible to be fully alive while sitting in a garden or playing on a field. Our sages say that there is no greater joy than the joy of being alive - that is, being completely engaged in one's life.

from the essay: Eighteenth of Elul

The Hebrew words for "new year" (*shana ḥadasha*) are a kind of oxymoron. "Shana" means something that repeats itself over and over, and "ḥadasha" means something new and different. Each year has basic cycles of repetition - autumn, winter, spring, summer, short days and long days, cold seasons and hot ones, rainy seasons and dry ones. There are always deviations from the norm, but we have no expectation of experiencing anything truly new in the cycle of events. Repetition is not limited to seasons of the year; it is a part of the structure of life itself. A person can spend his whole life repeating experiences without ever reaching a point of review, introspection, and judgment. For this kind of person, every year is another year of repetitive self-interest in a semi-wakeful state, a circle with no exit. In order to break free of this kind of automatic living, something must happen to change things, to awaken and disturb.

This is why the shofar is sounded! The call of the shofar is the voice of a silent scream; it is not pleasant to hear. It is wordless because there are no words that can express the inner voice of every human being. The blast of the shofar is sometimes a broken scream about what has been, and what has been lost. Sometimes it is a blast of warning, like an alarm. And sometimes it is also a promise that despite everything, it is still possible for life to be more than a repetition of what has been, a promise that in the cycle of time there is an opening for hope that the coming year will be truly new, a "*shana ḥadasha.*"

from the book: Change and Renewal

In Jewish as well as other cultures, the first day of the new year is a day of celebration and gaiety; it is a joyous entry into a new period of time. But the Jewish holiday of Rosh HaShana is more than just a joyous date marking the passage of time. It has a much more profound significance; there is an intrinsic relationship between the optimism associated with beginning a new year, and the solemnity of judgment about the old one. It is a day in which all of the trials and tribulations of the previous year are reviewed and hopefully rectified. Rosh HaShana is more than just the beginning of the new year; it also commemorates the first day of creation. Every year, on Rosh HaShana, the Holy One, blessed be He, decides whether or not the entire world should be allowed to continue.

It is a day of judgment, and the fate of the world hangs in the balance. The question that must be answered is: Did the past year justify its existence? The question that follows is even more poignant: Is justification of the past year sufficient reason to continue the "experiment" for another year? Beginning with creation and up until this point in time, the status of every year has been reviewed. Rosh HaShana is the point in time that connects what was with what will be.

from the book: Radiance of the King

Time

No two moments in time are exactly alike, just as no two people are exactly alike and no two places can be exactly alike. On a clock, time is divided into equal units; we imagine that one second is the same as the next. But this way of thinking is completely external to the nature of time. One can look at space in the same way, as when a place is defined only by its measurements. Distance can be the same, but every kilometer is actually unique; one kilometer can be mountainous, another can measure a body of water. One cannot do on a mountain range what one can do in the sea. Of the multitude of stars in the sky, it is written: "the Holy One, blessed be He, counts each star and gives it a name." Each and every star has its own name and its own identity.

It is also possible to count human beings - two people, one hundred people, one million people - and this number does have a literal meaning. But each person is an individual unlike any other. This is how we must see time. Every unit of time is an entity in and of itself, a unique moment of existence, a moment of meaning, a moment that has a beginning and an end, a moment that is born and dies, a moment that never was before and will never come again.

from the book: Commentary on the Tanya

One of the most important sentences written by our sages about the holidays is: "In every generation a man must see himself as if he too came out of Egypt." This approach gives us a new tool for understanding the holidays. By moving historical events into the realm of the personal, the three holidays (Passover, Shavuot, and Sukkot) become levels of spiritual development.

The first level is the exodus from Egypt (Passover). It represents coming out of a physical and spiritual vacuum, and moving on toward the unknown. Nothing can compare to the spiritual burden a person carries when making that fateful decision. One enters a desert devoid of content, and subsists on "the bread of affliction." It is impossible to take true sustenance from this kind of spiritual arousal. Only after continuing on a path that began in ignorance can one become aware that there are well-defined laws to guide the rest of the journey. A person can then begin to see the road ahead with clarity, and define the goal and true purpose of the journey.

The second level, receiving the Torah (Shavuot), refers to the time when one connects to, and takes on, the journey as a whole. While this represents a spiritual and intellectual resolution, it is not accompanied by internal tranquility. Receiving the Torah is characterized by a heightened feeling of yearning, and by a storm of other feelings. It is hard to absorb so much information that is close to the heart but new to the soul. A person can feel as if a mountain is hanging over his head ("*kafa aleihem hahar kegigit*"). That is why the making of a "golden calf" often follows receiving the Torah. It is sometimes a reaction to taking on so much unfamiliar content - an expression of the difficulty involved in absorbing and assimilating the unaccustomed into one's life.

Only after a prolonged interval of adjustment to the new path can a person begin to feel some degree of spiritual peace. The next holiday (Sukkot) is a time when it becomes possible to harvest all that has been cultivated and to enjoy the fruits of one's labors in an atmosphere of serenity and personal happiness. This reward is accessible to everyone.

from the essay: The Origin of the Beginning

As the new year approaches and we review the past year, we must remember that the Holy One, blessed be He, gave us the year and expects us to return it - every day, every hour of it. What are we supposed to return? More than we received. Time was given to us in order to improve upon it. Some people waste a day here and there, and return a year full of holes. Some return only a few months, or even a few days, or maybe just an hour or two. There is probably no way to correct this. It is possible to rectify almost everything that occurs in the realm of time, but it is impossible to "return" time itself. All we can do is take it upon ourselves, looking forward, to make every second count doubly.

from the essay: On Our Sin of Lost Time

Torah

The Torah enables us to relate and connect to the Holy One, blessed be He. It guides us to a path in life in this world. The intent of Torah is not to negate our world but to show us the way to erect and stabilize it, so it can bring forth its own light and reveal what it can and must be. Torah was also given to us to learn and question and debate. Engaging in Torah study is more than a heavenly gift; it becomes heaven itself, a ray of light from the Source of light.

from the essay: The Rebbe, Thirty Years of Leadership

Our sages have said that the Holy One, blessed be He, looked into the Torah and made the world accordingly. That is to say, the Torah is a blueprint for the inner structure of the world; the Torah and the world are forever intertwined. Torah expresses the inner will, the direction, and the relationship between the Holy One, blessed be He, and the world; the world is the concrete, material expression of His will.

Because of this, engaging in Torah study - emotionally as well as intellectually - gives us a way to identify with the desire of the Holy One, blessed be He. On an even deeper level, it enables us to participate in the delight of what can be called "a divine dream." A person who opens the Torah delves into it and learns. When thinking about it, he enters into a kind of partnership with the Holy One, blessed be He, in the planning and development of an idea. A human being can participate in realizing a "divine dream" about the way human beings and the world should be.

from the book: The Thirteen Petalled Rose

Torah

When all of the commandments of the Torah plus all of the customs and rituals that comprise observance are added together, their sum total reaches into the thousands. Everything must be done at the right time and in the right place and with the right intent. Add to this the huge number of rulings addressing questions on how commandments must be performed. The sheer multitude of details can be overwhelming, even frightening, when each one is seen as an isolated obligation, disconnected from the whole. From that perspective, the commandments of the Torah can appear to be a vast, almost absurd collection of detail upon tiny detail - complicated, excessive, and oppressive. Whoever sees them in this way can feel burdened and become estranged.

The truth is that these details are not separate from each other. When a person sees a tree as a whole, rather than looking at each leaf and bud as a separate entity, all of the details become integral parts of the life of the tree; large branches grow smaller offshoots, twigs and leaves and buds. When a person comprehends the life of the tree, and when he identifies the foundation of all of the parts, the details are no longer burdensome. The minutiae become parts of a single unified system of life.

from the book: The Thirteen Petalled Rose

Although the laws of the Torah are not presented in a way that can be applied in all possible circumstances, their teaching and meaning remain true for all situations in the world. The more deeply a person identifies with Torah, the more he understands its wide - ranging application. Broader application does not mean making the laws more difficult to observe by adding restrictions based on time or place, for example. It also does not mean idealizing observance so that only a "nazir," or someone who separates himself from ordinary life, can obey them. The opposite is true. Broader application means interpreting the laws in a practical way, so that they can be applied to real circumstances in the lives of real people - in the minutiae of personal life as it is lived. This overarching application of the laws begins with major decisions that a person makes in life, and ends with details that may seem to be insignificant.

from the book: The Thirteen Petalled Rose

Observance of most commandments involves a material act, or physical work. Torah study, on the other hand, falls into the category of spiritual work. If one sees prayer as the "work of the heart," then Torah study can be seen as "work of the brain." The purpose of ritual observance is to enable a connection to be made; it also involves an attempt to emulate the actions of the Holy One, blessed be He. Torah study achieves both of these aims. When a person does the "work of the brain" by sitting and learning Torah, a connection is created between the human mind and the thoughts of the Holy One, blessed be He, as they find expression in the Torah. Our sages have said that when a person reads Torah, the Holy One, blessed be He, reads it along with him. Torah study is a way in which a person creates an intimate connection with the Holy One, blessed be He; it is as if they are "on the same page."

from the essay: On Learning Torah

The basic definition of Torah is that it is the Torah of God; it is not the personal Torah of an individual. Because of this, the Torah, like God, has no bounds and cannot be limited. A person can never limit or restrict the Torah. If this were to occur, Torah would no longer be the Torah of God; the stamp of a person would be on the part of the Torah that happens to agree with his views. God's Torah cannot be realized in that way. The only way to "receive" the Torah is to become open to everything within it. A person must approach Torah without preconceived ideas about what he is capable of, or what he is willing or not willing to absorb based on individual tastes and preferences. Only then can the Torah be received.

from the book: Change and Renewal

Religion, in general, can be seen as a framework that brings order to that part of life related to serving God. But the Jewish religion, which is rooted in the Torah, cannot be confined to just one part of life. The practice of Judaism brings all aspects of a person's life - as well as that of the Jewish people as a whole - into a single, unified structure. That is why the Torah includes more than just instruction about the religious requirements of an individual (acts between man and God), or society (between man and man). The Torah includes, among other things, history, poetry, ethical guidance, prophesy, elements of permanence, as well as elements of wonder and doubt. All of these components comprise a single entity that cannot be divided.

Confining Torah to religious observance alone is destructive and heretical, as it nullifies the significance of Torah in one's life. Judaism differs from other religions of the world. A Jew is expected to build his entire life in a specific way so that life and Torah are inseparable.

from the book: Change and Renewal

Torah

Is it ever possible to finish learning the Torah? Events marking the completion of a section of the Talmud emphasize that every completion is not a true end to the learning of that portion, but rather a kind of pause, like a period at the end of a sentence. The celebration acknowledges that one can now go on to learning other sections and books. But it also emphasizes that the learning of that particular section has not ended. The most important words in the ceremony may be "*hadran alakh masekhet*," Aramaic for "we will return to you" - a promise that we will come back to that same portion and learn it again and again, even if we already know every word of it by heart. It is incumbent on us to return to it because each time any portion of Torah is learned, a different facet can be revealed.

At the completion of a section of Talmud, we not only say that we will return to it; we also say "*vehadrakh alan*" - it will return to us; it will be revealed to us. This may happen on the second learning and it may happen on the hundredth. Because of this, every "completion" of any section of Torah is just a temporary pause, after which we must go back and learn it all again, from the beginning.

from the essay: On Completion of the Torah

Prayer

The Rambam defines the commandment to pray as simply an obligation to serve God with one's heart. He goes on to say that there are no specific times or templates for prayer in the Torah; every moment is a moment of prayer and any form of prayer is acceptable. What then is prayer, according to the Torah? It seems to be that fragment of time in which a human being turns to the Holy One, blessed be He. It is the turning, rather than the words, that make it a prayer. Once, when international phone calls were very expensive, people traveling abroad would call home, let the phone ring once or twice, and then hang up. It was a sign to the family that all was well with the traveler. The type of prayer described in the Torah is like that. A connection is made; words are not necessary. The world can be changed in all possible ways when this kind of contact is initiated. Turning toward the Holy One, blessed be He, essentially creates the world anew.

from the essay: Repentance (Teshuva) Preceded Creation of the World

Sometimes when we pray, we hope that a true connection, an awakening and awareness, will be made at the beginning of the prayer and carry us like a wave until the end. Some things do work that way, but there are also many things that do not. Fluorescent light, for example, does not flow in a steady stream; it oscillates, back and forth. Prayer also does not have a stable, unidirectional flow. Prayer is characterized by movement that goes back and forth; there is trial and error in the attempt to gain ground. Little by little, the prayer begins to flow and gain momentum. It can be compared to an engine that has to be pumped again and again to get it going. The engine does not necessarily start on the first try; there are fits and starts. One must try again and again until the connection is made.

from the essay: A Gift from Above

Prayer

How should one approach prayer? How does one do "the work of the heart" that opens a soul to prayer, with understanding and true feeling? Given the nature of things, there is no set formula that can be relied upon to get a person truly ready to pray. Still, there are ways that can help, even if they do not provide a definite answer. A simple way that is possibly the most natural way, is to pray the way we disagree: someone says a word, another responds. Soon the exchange is heated. No preparation is necessary; one merely has to open the prayer book and begin to engage with intent and knowledge. In time, with continued perseverance and effort, something can happen to make the barrier between the "I" and the prayer begin to disappear. In one time out of many, in one particular prayer, or even in one letter, the prayer book stops being a book that I am reading, and starts being a book that I am in, a book about me.

from the book: The Thirteen Petalled Rose

Prayer has many facets, one of them being a potential for renewal. Prayer is not and should not be exactly the same today as it was yesterday, any more than a person is exactly the same from one day to the next. As much as possible, one must try to make one's daily prayers into an entirely new world, one that is not fixed eternally. It is incumbent on us to reveal new aspects of prayer every time we pray. It has been said that "the prayer of one who prays by rote is not an entreaty." A prayer that has become repetitive and unchanging is a flawed prayer. Prayer must always involve movement.

from the essay: Life in the Present

A great deal is said about how a person should make his prayers "new." We are exhorted in the book of Psalms (Tehillim) to "Sing to God a new song"; this is usually not meant to be taken literally. We are being challenged to think about how to say a familiar prayer over and over again. A programmed machine cannot sing a new song, but a human being can. Prayer, like other things repeated on a daily basis, can be renewed each day because one's life is different today from yesterday. Major changes are not necessary, and would be wrong. The right kind of change in a prayer stems from deep within one's soul, based on experiences that have made an impact on one's life. These need not be exceptional adventures; routine events also affect life experience. Are any two days ever the same?

When looking into a kaleidoscope, one can see a magical world of changing shapes and colors. Entirely new designs can be created by slight movement of a few pieces of colored glass. There must be millions of possible designs in every kaleidoscope - more than the number of prayers a person can pray in a lifetime. Anyone who has difficulty renewing his prayers should peer into his kaleidoscope once again.

from the essay: Renewal of Prayer

The true value of prayer is not measured by how much a person cries, or how frequently he bows, or even by how much he feels, but rather by how much is left of the experience afterward. The Kotzker Rebbe interprets the phrase from the prayer "*Yishtabaḥ*" to mean "He who selects what remains of the song" ("*haboḥer b'shayarei zimra*") instead of "He who selects the songs" ("*haboḥer b'shirei zimra*"). If one's feelings are true, they remain so after the prayer is over. These "remains" are not necessarily conscious, or even felt. They are just an impression that something has transpired. A true sign that something has remained of the prayer is a change within the person; that change proves that the experience was real.

from the book: The Thirteen Petalled Rose

When praying, one flows with the movement of the prayer as it goes from one blessing to another and one hymn to the next. Each transition is a passage from one world to another. One moves with the prayer as a traveler on a train, from one landscape to the next, one climate to another. In prayer, a person is on Mount Moriah, then at the sacrifice of Isaac, then on the Temple mount offering sacrifices, then high in the heavens praising God with the sun and the moon, with creatures of the depths, in fire and hail, then at the Red Sea singing the song of Moses, then with angels, singing "holy, holy, holy" amid the din of Seraphim, then committing his soul with absolute devotion to love the "One."

This is prayer at its most complete, when the words of the prayer and the inner experience of the person praying are one and the same. People truly at prayer can be compared to those dancing to a melody, when the dance and the melody are inseparable and it is impossible to tell which came first. Prayer is like that, even though one part is ritually organized and the other part occurs within a person's heart. Both are intertwined, both have the same words, and both follow the same rhythm.

from the essay: To Pray with Innocence

Prayer

One has to flow with prayer the way one flows with music. A symphony has different parts, some joyful, some sad; it elicits different feelings from one movement to the next. This is how one must follow the prayerbook. Similarly, just as a person on a hike reacts differently to the changing environment, a person going from one world to another in prayer is obligated to adjust and to change. Walking through an open field is different from passing under a waterfall, or climbing on rocks. Though standing still in prayer, one must try to have a different inner experience for each part of the prayer as a whole.

The last psalm in the book of Psalms, recited daily, exhorts us to "Praise God with tambourines, praise Him with stringed instruments," etc. What is most interesting about this psalm is that every verse describes a different musical instrument – harp, lyre, timbrel, shofar, cymbals. Each one makes a completely different sound; each has its own voice. In prayer, a person must want to sing to God with all of these instruments and voices.

Imagine that they all are a part of the same little orchestra, playing together without diss nance. Am I capable, deep within, of feeling and hearing each distinct voice? More importantly: Am I capable of playing them all within me at the same time? This takes work; this is the work of prayer.

from the essay: To Pray with Innocence

Repentance

Repentance

Teshuva (repentance) encompasses an entire world, one that is based on two contradictory, yet complementary perceptions On one hand, teshuva is exceedingly difficult - there is nothing harder, as it necessitates change, reversal, and assuming a new identity. On the other hand, there is nothing simpler to accomplish; the tiniest fraction of a turn, the most minute change in direction, is enough to place a person in the realm of teshuva.

from the essay: Teshuva, a Return to the Source

The essential thing to try to understand about teshuva is that it defies nature as we know it. There are things in nature that we cannot encounter without damage. I cannot put my hand in fire without getting burned; I cannot lie down in snow, unprotected, without freezing. Similarly, I cannot sin without the sin becoming a part of my soul and changing it. A sin can cause a stain that alters an entire spiritual world. In the material world, there is no turning back. I cannot say - sorry, I made a mistake, I didn't mean to jump off the roof. After the fact, it is impossible to change the reality of the jump.

In that sense, teshuva remains completely outside the natural order of the world. Every act of teshuva rewrites the past; it is not merely a resolution to start a new day or turn over a new leaf. Teshuva can change yesterday, last week, the past year, and past decades. What has been done ceases to be; what has not been done becomes as if it had been done. This is the paradox, the miracle of teshuva. A person can change the course of his life, not only looking forward with resolutions, but looking backward as well.

from the essay: The Cycle of the Year

It is possible for a person to feel that he has done nothing wrong, even if reality contradicts this impression. This is the greatest obstacle to repentance: If one thinks – there is nothing wrong with me that is not wrong with society as a whole, with my family, with God, etc., etc.

Feelings of self-satisfaction regarding one's spiritual and moral state are not necessarily based on an objective reality. A person can be seen by many as a sinner and evildoer, and still see himself as innocent and completely in the right. Someone in this frame of mind can never repent. In contrast, a person who is honest and pure can still perceive deficiencies within. For this kind of person, the gates of repentance remain open.

from the essay: Teshuva, a Return to the Source

One who seeks to do teshuva needs to acknowledge that the act of repentance must be irreversible. True repentance is comparable to a circumcision, where something is cut off, discarded, and leaves a scar. A few good lawyers can invalidate a contract, but a foreskin, once excised, remains cut off forever.

Every time a person remembers his desire to change course and repent, a feeling should arise within that gives him no rest and does not allow him to revert to past behavior. This decision needs to push him forward to progress, step by step. Once accomplished, the act of repentance must remain valid, relevant, and forever unforgotten. It is all about the decision, and the movement forward. A person can learn and pray a great deal, but if nothing comes of this genuine determination to change, all of the learning and prayer are no more than a collection of details, destined to fade away and leave no lasting impression. Teshuva must be a commitment, a covenant.

from the essay: Breathing Life into Elul

Repentance

Teshuva begins with thoughts and feelings, but the first sign of it is with words, like the *Seliḥot* said during the ten days of repentance between Rosh HaShana and Yom Kippur. These words are a gateway into the void, into an emptiness that contains everything; they are an entrance into a space that allow us to change.

Though all life was created by God, only human beings, by our words and deeds, can enact the change and the repair that the world needs. The Holy One, blessed be He, created the world so that it could change; he gave human beings the desire, ability, and the madness needed to execute these changes.

from the essay: Creation and Change – in Word and in Deed

One's distance from the Holy One, blessed be He, is not a physical one and cannot be measured in any way; it is rather one of relationship. When a person takes a wrong path in life, he is, in a sense, turning his back on God; his inner soul is drawn toward other objectives and headed in a different direction. That is why the basic element of teshuva is the turning point, the instant a person decides to alter the direction of his life, to turn away from things he had desired and pursued, and to redirect himself and his desires to the Holy One, blessed be He. The turning point is the defining moment of teshuva.

from the book: The Thirteen Petalled Rose

In the Jewish world view, there is almost no striving to reach inner peace. The feeling of having "arrived" at the goal negates the possibility to continue. This kind of ideal is based on the assumption that it is possible to reach infinity with a finite number of steps. Since the essence of God is infinite, any attempt to get closer to God must be endless. When a person does teshuva, a never-ending path toward holiness lies ahead, even if one has advanced significantly.

Only when looking back can a person see the distance traveled and appreciate the progress made, how far he has come. That is why the result of teshuva is never accompanied by a feeling of self-satisfaction, wholeness, or completion. Progress in teshuva leads to a striving for additional effort.

from the book: The Thirteen Petalled Rose

The voice of God calls to each and every Jew with a promise: "Return to Me and I will return to you." Both the call and its answer come from God alone. God is telling us that He is present, and calling on each one of us to return to Him, to become closer to Him, to find shelter under His wings. This same call holds true for those who are close and for those most distant. There is no such thing as being too distant from God to hear His call. It can be heard even by those who, in their darkest moments, imagine themselves to be completely disconnected from Him. Even to them, God promises the light of forgiveness, abundant loving-kindness, and the wholeness that comes with being one with God.

from the essay: Return, Children

Education

Judaism recognizes that there is evil in this world. Its goal is to change the world by replacing evil with good; the purpose of Jewish education is to teach us how to do so. This change begins with internal, spiritual self-correction. That can, in turn, enable societal and economic change to blossom. On that basis, real and permanent correction can take place and be sustained. When the Almighty is recognized as King by a society that yearns for a kingdom of heaven, for rulership and governance that is as good as humanly possible, then true correction of our world also becomes possible.

from the essay: To Repair the World with a Kingdom of Heaven

Many educational strategies emphasize the importance of making each and every subject "relevant." This is a serious mistake. Teachers, and sometimes parents as well, are convinced that this approach intensifies and deepens a child's desire to learn. What it actually does do is destroy curiosity, which is much more important than "relevance." Interest in things that have no immediate or even long-term significance is a part of what makes us uniquely human. Why do we bother to learn laws that relate to events of the past, of which we may know little?

Why do we bother to teach a child things that even the Talmud admits have never been and may never be? We devote time to these things because we are in search of knowledge for its own sake, not only for its practical application.

Admittedly, curiosity varies - bubbling over in some people and dormant in others. But learning for the sake of learning is not just encouraged in Judaism, it is a required part of observance.The sheer number of courses and lectures available to observant Jews is unmatched by other faith communities anywhere else in the world.

In my opinion, learning Torah for its own sake enables a person to reach a higher level than angels, who lack even a modicum of curiosity, as they already know everything. Human beings "created in the image of God" are unique in that they are the only creatures in the universe who have been given any curiosity whatsoever. Other creatures learn what they need to know in order to survive.

from the essay: Curiosity

In today's modern era, schools and teachers have two essential responsibilities that no book or digital platform can ever accomplish. The first is to teach students how to learn, the second is to help shape the student's personality. Teaching a student how to learn is completely different from the transmission of knowledge. A trainer teaches an athlete to run but does not run for him. This holds true for transmission of all kinds of knowledge. To truly teach is to "get into the student's head," to try to understand why he is having trouble with specific topics, and to help him figure out how to overcome these difficulties.

The second responsibility of a teacher toward a student is to influence the development of the student's personality. This is a far greater educational accomplishment than any academic achievement. A good teacher helps a student learn how to learn; a great teacher teaches the student how to be what is called in Yiddish a "mensch" - a human being. Turning a child into a mensch is the greatest accomplishment a teacher can achieve. It falls into the realm of "walking in His path." The teacher, like the Creator Himself, fashions a human being.

from the essay: Building Character

Our future teachers must be talented and passionate about their work. Hiring teachers only because they can transmit required material or keep a class in order should be unacceptable. It is like hiring them because they would like a job with long summer breaks. From a societal perspective, there is an essential need to recognize the critical importance of attracting the best and the brightest among us to become teachers. A body with an impaired nervous system can still grow, but it cannot function normally. A society whose teachers lack the necessary abilities is in real danger. The ability to function, and certainly to prepare for the future, whatever may come, is based on those who transmit a spiritual lifeline from one generation to the next.

This is true for those who teach at every level of education, starting with the earliest grades of elementary school. Unsatisfactory educators can cause crises that can be literally life threatening. Those who truly want the good of society must remember that the best of the best should be encouraged to enter the teaching profession. In time, society will also compensate these teachers as they deserve to be compensated. But the need for these teachers is current, urgent, and of critical importance, now.

from the essay: The Best Should Teach

A teacher occupies a unique and crucial role among professions, and enables the continuity of humanity by helping students of the present connect to knowledge of the past. At the same time, a teacher paves the groundwork for the future. Students are not just receptacles of information; they internalize it, and carry it forward with them as they grow. The spiritual role of a teacher can be compared to the physical role of parents. Biological parents transmit genetic information to their children, connecting past, present, and possibly future; teachers do this spiritually.

This role is of paramount importance to our society, as a teacher holds human continuity and hope in his hands. This job should be given to people who are most deserving and most capable of fulfilling this critical task.

from the essay: The Best Should Teach

Society as a whole needs great teachers, as teachers pass information from one generation to the next, from the past to the present and forward into the future. Any defect in their ability to do so is not just the personal problem of a given teacher, school, or even policy. It is the problem of humanity, and it has far-reaching consequences.

Enabling a given generation to absorb the message of the past is only half of the task; teachers must also show students how to incorporate what they have learned and build on it. Animals learn instinctively; information necessary for survival is passed wordlessly from one generation to the next. Human beings also know some things by instinct, but in order for them to reach the level of knowledge of the preceding generation, active learning is critical. In order to stand on their own two feet, human beings cannot rely solely on instinct.

from the essay: The Best Should Teach

In Judaism, great education is rooted in questioning; it is more than just transmission of knowledge. The entire Talmud is based on questions and the concerns, arguments, and problems of those who are learning.There is no language that has as many words for "question" as the Hebrew-Aramaic of the Talmud. There are different words for different types of questions, for the meaning of a question, and for the urgency of a question. Dissection of this terminology is not irrelevant. It draws attention to the difference between the usual approach to higher education, where students must demonstrate some proficiency in a subject in order to take a particular class, and Talmud study.

The task of a teacher in Judaism is to try to show students all of the different ways in which they can question the material. What is a student allowed to ask? The answer is: anything! Despite the fact that no subject is off limits, our houses of study, for generations, were famous for their clean language.

Jewish institutions of higher learning require only that the question be a good one and that the discussion about it be appropriate. And some questions need to be dealt with in small groups or individually.

The task of the student is to raise questions and attack a problem from all directions; the more exhaustive the approach, the better. The entire talmudic literature is based on the expectation that questions can and will be asked, even though answers might not always be possible. This is what is called learning: asking the question and attempting to come to an answer.

from the essay: Jewish Education in the Ancient World

Is it possible to teach children to be good people? There are many places that make a conscious attempt to do so, either with an integrated educational policy or in specially dedicated parts of the curriculum. The effort to foster goodness is, in itself, worthwhile and positive. Children exposed to examples of good people from the past and present are given models they can emulate. Learning about the kind of behavior that is deserving of esteem and praise can be internalized. This education may not fully succeed. But the child who grows up with it may one day say to himself: Even if I may not be a good person, at least I know how to recognize and appreciate goodness.

from the essay: Good People

Connections

Abraham is not revealed to us as a man who acts single-handedly, and Sarah is not revealed to us as just the woman by his side. Abraham and Sarah are portrayed in the Torah as a unit, as equals. When Abram's name is changed to Abraham - an occurrence of major significance - Sarai's name is also changed, to Sarah. This is the only time that the Torah notes a change in the name of a woman. Changing a name has far-reaching consequences, and hints at the transformation of the entire course of one's life - a fundamental change in one's existence. Parallel changes in the names of both Abraham and Sarah signify that they are a unit, and that their mission in life is as a couple on equal footing.

from the book: Women in the Bible

A true meeting of souls might possibly be the most intimate type of connection - physical or spiritual - that two people can make. Sometimes, but not always, this kind of profound connection exists in a couple, or as part of a friendship; it can also exist between a teacher and student, Rebbe and hasid, tzaddik and disciple. Two souls connected in this way are called "soulmates." These connections, which are not all that rare, have great power. They result in a level of intimacy that is not possible to achieve in any way other than by revealing a deeply veiled part of the soul.

People often yearn for this kind of closeness, but it rarely happens without great effort. Even relationships between people who are extremely involved in each other's lives, like members of the same family, do not necessarily reach this degree of depth. There must be a willingness on both sides to expose one's deepest truths, as well as the desire and motivation to create an intimate bond. Even then, the effort does not always succeed. Fortunate is the person who is able to make this kind of connection with a true "soulmate."

from the essay: The Soul

Connections

In the commandment to "love another as thyself," what does "as thyself" add? It adds that even though I may have two left hands, or see a crooked smile or fishy eyes when I look in the mirror, and even though others may be prettier or better or smarter than I am, I still basically love myself. Simply put, "as thyself" means that just as I am willing to tolerate my own imperfections, I must try to be willing to tolerate those of others.

I know less about others than I do about myself, and certainly much more about myself than others know about me. I know all about the forbidden deeds I should not have done, all about the forbidden words I should not have spoken, and all about the forbidden or just polluted thoughts that should not have crossed my mind. I know that I need to improve yet I still love myself.

When I am commanded to "love another as myself," I am commanded to love others, or at least not to hate them, even when I know that they are deserving of rebuke. I must try to achieve a balance between "do not hate your brother in your heart" and "admonish and reprove." The challenge is how to navigate that fine line, how to point out bad behavior in others without hatred, and with the same compassion and tolerance that you show yourself.

from the essay: The Tenth of Shevat

Connections

When a slight, temporary partition is built in a country, it can turn into a massive solid wall. A little crack in the road can become an abyss that cannot be bridged.

People can become divided by barriers and chasms – left and right, religious and secular. And these groups themselves can then be subdivided further. What all of the factions have in common is a great deal of hostility, anger, and alienation in particular. The farther apart they are from each other, the farther they are from actual facts on the ground, the greater the differences can become. This huge gap in political and religious persuasions threatens to swallow up everything held in common. The more people speak about these differences, the more they become convinced that they are too profound to be reconciled. This is true even for those who know that issues are oversimplified when portrayed as having just two opposing sides. The reality is much more complicated, and the differences are much less extreme.

The only advice that can possibly forestall the situation from worsening is simple: Try not to build the partition in the first place, even if it seems necessary. Try not to be divisive. Think long and hard before saying or doing anything that can be perceived as hostile. If not, these partitions will grow into walls of steel that future generations will have to work very hard to dismantle.

from the essay: The Land Where Walls Can Grow

The reason a person has two eyes is not because two eyes can see farther than one, but because each eye sees things from a different perspective. By doing so, and only by doing so, it is possible to perceive depth and to assess distance. When a person tries to evaluate his own self by looking within, he lacks perspective through no fault of his own; he is only capable of seeing things from one point of view. It does not matter whether he looks from the bottom up, and sees himself as greater than he actually is, or from the top down, and sees himself as smaller than he actually is. Either way, his view is distorted.

Because of this, and specifically when dealing with matters of one's soul, it is good for a person to turn to others for help. This is not necessarily because another person is wiser; it is just because someone else sees things from a different perspective. Our sages tell us that even the wisest of men need someone to enable them to see the big picture with a greater degree of truth.

from the essay: When the Police Force Investigates Itself

Love of one's fellow man is basically characterized by the removal of barriers that separate one person from another; it is an attachment of hearts. This definition of love never includes force, subservience, or the blurring of the independence of an individual. This mutual flow of love does not change either person; rather it tries to change his place. When two people love each other, screens between them are removed and each individual grows and develops spiritually.

from the essay: Love of Israel

Unity is not created by placing one thing next to another. To build a unified society that is not just a collection of a thousand separate parts, one must have a structure of connectivity that works even if the numbers grow to include millions of individuals. Only when the construct itself unifies people can a truly intact society be built. Without this structure it is impossible to create something whole.

Things thrown together into a drawer, with the thought that each one might be needed at some point, does not unify them. When building a society, the search for common ground is critical. Sometimes people share a yearning for something from their past. Sometimes they share a search for their souls. Sometimes they share a dream.

from the essay: The Individual and Society

When a person greets a friend with "Shalom," the word is more than just a blessing that his friend be free of trouble - that he not be robbed, for example. It is a blessing for personal wholeness, for harmony with himself and with the world. Since ancient times it has been well known that peace entails more than just a lack of enmity. Peace necessitates a kind of fusion, an internal chemistry that enables two sides to move forward together.

This very serious requirement asks a great deal of each side. It means giving up some independence, or even changing aspects of one's identity. When "side A" and "side B" want to be at peace, they stop being what they were and become an entirely new entity. This is as true for peace between married couples as it is for nations, and as it is for the proverbial wolf and lamb.

from the essay: Peace

Love for the Jewish People

From a uniquely Jewish perspective, the Jewish people can be seen as a family rather than as a nation. This is not only true because of our shared past; seeing us as a family helps to resolve the ongoing question of "who is a Jew."

The "House of Jacob" and the "House of Israel" are both broad terms reflecting the identity of one connected family. A family is not defined purely by cultural connections or geographic location. Being born into a given family is also not a choice. A person may dislike family members, and even behave with active hostility toward them. But the bond of their shared inheritance and identity is one that cannot be broken.

from the essay: What Is a Jew

From a psychosocial aspect based solidly on theology, the Jewish people are a family, with all of the messiness, bickering, and even bloody fighting that can occur within families. Does a quarrel between brothers mean they are no longer brothers? Of course not. Members of a family are bound together physically and emotionally. It is not uncommon or unexpected for there to be disagreements between them that cannot be resolved without passion. Members of a family lack the objectivity of distance. In nature, the most violent fights occur between members of the same species. Even Isaiah, in his prophecy of a future when "wolf and lamb will live together," did not promise that two lambs could live together in peace. Fights are unpleasant and occasionally dangerous, but they fall within the norm of family relations.

It is when family members begin to see brothers and sisters as "others" that things become treacherous. Seeing family members as complete strangers falls way beyond the norm of a family disagreement. It implies the kind of terrifying acceptance experienced after the death of a loved one. This attitude of "there is no longer anyone to talk to" is, in my opinion, the most dangerous threat to our existence as a people.

from the essay: Brotherhood

The commandment to love one's fellow Jew (*ahavat Yisrael*) obligates us to see each and every Jew, wherever he may be, whatever her status, as a vehicle of blessing. This love does not stem from a person's true worth or value to society. It has to be felt toward every person, whether worthy of esteem or not. It has to be felt even toward people whose choices and paths and methods we are obligated to oppose. It is a mitzva to love them even at the time of their misbehavior, and never to forget the light of the soul even when it is occluded by evil or boorishness.

from the essay: The Lubavitcher Rebbe

In contrast to the love that two people have for each other - that is, a love based on those two individuals - the love of one's fellow Jew stems from a shared love of God and His Torah. It is Torah that essentially made us into a nation, into the "people of the Book." It is the Torah that kept us together all these years, despite misfortune, exile, and degradation. The Torah that made us into a nation is the Torah that guards us and ensures our survival as a nation. The Torah is the focal point of all components of Jewish identity; it is the high ideal on which the love of one's fellow Jew is based.

from the essay: The Love of One's Fellow Jew

The relationship between one Jew and another can be compared to the way in which different parts of a single body connect with each other. The term "one body" in modern parlance refers to a single organic entity, an interrelated system that is more than just a collection of different parts. Six hundred chairs in one place are not an organic system. But six hundred and thirteen parts of a human body are an organic system, as are six hundred and thirteen commandments. An organic system can be defined as follows: First - all of the parts are integral to the functioning of the system as a whole; they cannot be added to, or removed arbitrarily. Second - individual parts relate to each other as well as to the system. Third - each part is necessary for the functioning of the whole. When seen in this light, the Jewish people comprise one organic system. Every individual is vital to all of the others. Another's needs, pains, or illnesses cannot be ignored any more than a head can ignore a bleeding finger.

Love of one's fellow Jew is not defined emotionally; it means taking responsibility and refusing to be oblivious to the needs of others. A Jew cannot say: "I don't care," and ignore his fellow Jew. His problem is your problem.

from the book: Commentary on the Tanya

For many generations, the saying, "a Jewish sinner remains a Jew," has been the principle on which "love of one's fellow Jew" is based. It means that a Jew cannot disconnect from his people even if he feels completely detached from God and His commandments. One of the reasons the Hasidic movement had been so successful in reaching Jews of different levels of knowledge and observance was because it understood the meaning of "loving one's fellow Jew." From a halakhic standpoint, it is possible to take issue with this approach. How can you disregard a basic tenet of Judaism, the commandment to love God, and remain devoted to a seemingly lesser tenet, to love one's brother? How can you come to the defense of a Jew who ignores and rejects his Creator?

The answer becomes clear when one understands that this defense is based on the underlying belief that the soul of every Jew is inherently good. Misdeeds and sins, no matter how great, are like passing clouds that can temporarily occlude but can never obliterate the light that is present in every soul.

from the essay: The Love of One's Fellow Jew

The love of a fellow Jew is based on the assumption that one's own identity is part of a larger entity that includes many different elements and issues. My identity, as well as that of other Jews, is part of the whole that belongs to the Holy One, blessed be He. That is the reason I cannot give up on any part of this larger body. My willingness to give up on another Jew says more about the kind of person I am than it says about anyone else. Imagine a person looking at his own body and saying, "This finger is a bit crooked; I think I'll cut it off." A person who could say something like that is not rational.

from the essay: The Tenth of Shevat

There is a prayer that I see almost as a slogan: "Guardian of Israel, guard the remnant of Israel, so that those who say *Shema Yisrael* will not be lost." Guardian of Israel, guard us, so that we will remain connected as one, despite grievances, arguments, slaps in the face we may have received, or may not yet have received. Guard us so that we will feel like brothers, united in flesh and blood. The point is to see ourselves the way Jacob's sons did, in Genesis - "We are twelve brothers, sons of our father." Seen in this way, we remain brothers to the end.

from the essay: A Bone of My Bones

Freedom & Renewal

At the start of Yom Kippur, as evening descends and the holiday begins, the Kol Nidrei prayer is r cited. What does it mean when a person says, "All of my vows...are nullified"? It is a declaration. I am asserting that all of the limitations, definitions, and boundaries that I have created for myself this past year, as well as labels that might limit me in the future – all are canceled, null and void. My path is now free of past as well as future limitations.

from the book: Radiance of the King

Like other creatures, human beings have the ability to grow. Free will, on the other hand, is a quality unique to human beings, who share it (as if) with the Holy One, blessed be He. Free will enables us to shake the world. Other creatures behave as nature dictates. Planets, stars, suns, and moons follow their orbits. Only people have the ability to choose a path - between good and evil, right and wrong. Human beings were created for this reason: to be the dynamic element in a system that is programmed and static.

The changes we make in the material world are readily visible; the changes we make in higher spiritual worlds are just as real, but cannot be seen. Our fundamental job, the nature of our very existence, is to use free will to change the world, physically and spiritually.

from the essay: Prophecy

A person who is not autonomous is always at the mercy of external influences and stimuli. An autonomous person can live large or small, have times of success and times of failure, but does not allow these situations to derail him. He has chosen to follow a path, no matter how winding it turns out to be. And even with its ups and downs, he continues to move forward, directed toward a goal. What he must do remains clear.

from the essay: The Tenth of Shevat

Teshuva represents the pinnacle of human free will. It enables a person to let go of the burden of past life experiences and break the chain of events that have spun him around and led him to a place from which there seems to be no return and no exit. The very possibility that a person can get to the point of teshuva means that events that occurred on his winding path are not irreparable. A person can gain control of the direction and outcome of his journey. One's path in life is not predestined; it can be abandoned at will. Teshuva empowers a person to break free of a pattern where one thing leads to another, one deed enables another, and sin begets sin.

from the book: The Thirteen Petalled Rose

If freedom is defined as the absence of slavery, then emancipating a slave would make him free. This is not true; physical freedom alone does not make a person free. True freedom must include positive spiritual aspects - free will, identity, and goals. This applies to the lives of individual human beings as well as to the life of a nation. Animals born in captivity and held there for a prolonged period of time are subsequently unable to adjust to the freedom of life in the wild. Prolonged dependence on their handlers stifles the internal drive needed to function independently. They return in a matter of days to the captivity to which they had become habituated. And they return even if the master they had come to rely upon had been cruel. This can be even more true of human beings than it is of animals.

To be truly free, a person must have an independent identity, with self-driven goals that propel him forward on a path, d espite any difficulties that may arise.

from the essay: Freedom via Commandments

The very beginning of the ritual Jewish confession is: "We are not approaching You with arrogance or stubbornness by stating: 'O Lord our God, and God of our fathers, we are righteous and have not sinned.' But we and our fathers have sinned." When I beat my breast and say, "I have sinned, transgressed, and falsified," I am clearly speaking of my own sins. What right have I to drag my fathers into my confession?

The answer is that every group in our midst has its own "private" Shulhan Arukh (instructions on how commandments are observed). And in every "private" Shulḥan Arukh, the following comments can be found: "It is not our custom to observe the following laws. Such and such transgressions are not considered by us to be sins." And there is another list stating: "The following things are not thought by us to be commandments." As for the actual Shulḥan Arukh, what power does it have? From a practical standpoint, we live according to our family's or our congregation's own little Shulḥan Arukh. That is why, when asking someone, "How can you possibly do this or that?" the Shulhan Arukh clearly states that it is forbidden! The response is often an astonished reply: "Does it really matter if it's written in the Shulḥan Arukh? So many things are in that book!"

That is why, when I say, "we and our fathers have sinned," I am stating that I am willing, essentially, to begin a deeper and much more basic examination of my life and my values.

from the essay: But We and Our Fathers Have Sinned

In order to truly adopt a culture or religion, a person must be free to choose. It is impossible to make someone do this by force. External pressure, whether physical or spiritual, can, at most, bring about external connectedness. True spiritual connections can only be made when a person is absolutely free to ask questions and determine the direction of his own unique soul, in his own unique way. These are things no stranger can possibly access. To truly connect to a religious belief, freedom of thought and questioning are necessary. Yet without commitment, questions on their own can cause irreparable damage to one's soul.

Questions must be accompanied by a desire to hear answers. Internalizing and accepting the answers, and incorporating them into one's thoughts, feelings, and deeds is critical. It enables a person to feel whole – not in a sense of being complete, but in terms of having the potential to achieve wholeness.

from the essay: Goals and Trends in Religious Education

Leaving exile can enable a great many things, but on its own, it does not represent even the beginning of redemption. The many diverse trials that have occurred to the Jewish people on their external journey out of bondage toward freedom have not been sufficient to bring them to the point of true redemption. A slave can rebel, but if his nature and spirit remain unchanged, he remains a slave. Merely to have left the desert of other nations is not enough. In order to be free, the Jewish people must also regain their independent identity, character, spirit, way of thought, and way of life.

from the essay: From Slavery to Freedom

Exile & Redempion

Exile is a state of existence where one is acted upon - like a slave who must do the bidding of his master. Ever since the destruction of the Temple, every generation of the Jewish people has been in exile - influenced by forces at play in the external environment, as if pulled and dragged by others. In the portion of the Torah dealing with retribution, there is a curse: "He will be the head and you will be the tail." This is more than a curse; it is an insult. When a nation or an individual becomes a tail, others take the place of the head. Protracted exile and the accompanying metamorphosis of the entire Jewish people into a tail is a terrifying manifestation of the exile of God Himself (*Galut HaShekhina*).

from the essay: How Much Can We Endure

The question, "How can this be?" (*Eikha*), is not an attempt to clarify how or why destruction occurred, based on military, political, or historic analysis; it is not even an attempt to provide a moral explanation for the disaster. The question is an existential one about the present: How can the current situation even be possible? Posing the question in that way creates, on its own, a feeling of pain and loss.

The fact that lamentations are recited on a yearly basis, and the question "*Eikha*?" is a repeated refrain, means that we are not really whole or at peace with our current existence. In the book of Psalms, the psalmist says of the return to Zion: "As God brings us to Zion we are like dreamers." He is referring not to the dream of future redemption, but rather to the nightmare of past exile. Exile is understood as a prolonged horror that will end when the nation awakens and finds itself once again in authentic circumstances. Until this happens, we lament the current reality and we question, with incredulousness: "How can this be?"

from the book: Change and Renewal

Redemption follows exile, as day follows night. It is the natural next phase, even though it might seem to be an entirely new era. After the preparatory stage has been completed, exile is followed by redemption, just as sleep is followed by wakefulness. Seeds that grew and developed in a concealed manner during the hardship of exile bear fruit when it ends. The more difficult the challenge and the longer the exile, the loftier the redemption.

This step up must be preceded by a phase that involves reducing the importance of external conditions, and letting go of the need to understand everything. It is specifically in this kind of lowered state that a person, and a nation, are able to receive the flow of abundance from on high. By accepting a dream on faith, even when it might not be reality based, we are able to reach a higher level of existence.

from the essay: from Slavery to Freedom

The essential idea of the Messianic era is, first and foremost, the redemption of the Jewish people, the desire for a return to past glory, and renewal of the kingdom of Judah. The idea of Messianic times is actually broader than this; the redemption of the nation of Israel is just the first step in a comprehensive process that includes the redemption of the entire world.

The Messianic era will be more than just a new order in the political structure of the world. It will usher in a time when relationships between people, as well as the relationship between human beings and the Holy One, blessed be he, will change for the better. The essential structure and identity of the world in which we live will also improve. The arrival of the Messiah will usher in the beginning of a new world - one without war, without deprivation, and without physical or spiritual suffering.

from the essay: Messianic Complex

Belief in the coming of the Messiah is more than just an ethereal thought about a future loftier existence. This is unlike believing in the rewards of the soul in the World to Come. Belief in the Messiah is a practical belief that human beings have the ability to change this world. Implicit in this belief is the hope that this change will be accompanied by a reduction in difficulties and overall suffering.

Belief in the coming of the Messiah, and in our ability to hasten it, is essential to our identity as Jews. Part of our purpose and mandate as Jews is to be at the forefront of change to improve the world as a whole. A Jew must feel, even when he is not actively doing something, that deeds matter, that what one does can help to bring about positive change. The anticipation of the arrival of the Messiah is not just a passive hope; it is a desire that compels to action that can bring about the redemption of the world.

from the essay: Exile as Delusion

We need to paddle forward, one stroke at a time. We need to give it our all. Another stroke, another long glide. And we need to assist those who are struggling to keep up - be it physically or spiritually - because what awaits us is critical. The coming of the Messiah basically signifies the end of history as we know it. Human history is the story of endless suffering and conflict. The Messianic era will be a time when we will finally be able to live together in peace and security; there will be no going back to the ways of the past. This day is not far away; we must keep aiming to reach it, and keep believing that we can.

from the essay: The Captain

Our sages comment that in the statement "Do not harm my Messiahs," the Holy One, blessed be He, is referring to young schoolchildren as Messiahs. Older children might all like to grow up to be Messiahs, but kindergarten children are all little Messiahs - not because of their current abilities or even future potential - but because of the power of desire and belief, the power of a dream.

From a spiritual perspective, each and every Jew actually does have a Messianic spark. This, of course, does not mean that every Jew can be a Messiah – not potentially and certainly not actually – but a kind of spark does exist within. Part of our inherited identity from past leaders of the nation – Abraham, Isaac, and Jacob – lives on in us and can ignite the spark and impact the future. The ultimate Messiah will represent a true expression and unification of all the sparks of all of the Jews of all the preceding generations.

from the essay: Messianic Complex

The Jewish people are more than just a nation; they serve as the internal identity, or soul, of the world as a whole. The purpose of the Jewish people is to be like a seed planted in the earth, one that can direct its potential to grow into a great magnificent tree. Its function is to make the entire world more "Jewish" - that is, to help it become a world whose identity reflects God's will and embodies holiness.

The process of redemption from exile involves learning. The world must learn who it is, what its powers are, and the nature of its identity. In a certain way, this process can be compared to psychoanalysis. In its current state, the world is suffering from a spiritual illness; it mistakenly thinks that it has an existence that is separate and disconnected from its Creator. In order to heal, it must learn to recognize the truth - that all is Divine, that there is nothing besides Him. The role of the Jewish people is to bring about the healing of the world.

from the essay: On Exile and Redemption

Man & the World

To the best of my knowledge, the expression, "the shame of hunger," does not exist in any language other than Hebrew. It refers to the profound shame that should be felt by members of a society that is willing to allow its people to go hungry. A community is forbidden to tolerate hunger in its midst. The embarrassment felt by those who are actually hungry is mild in comparison. It is written that in days to come, "the shame of His people will be removed from all of the land." This means that, in a future time, no individual or community will ever have to feel "the shame of hunger," as there will no longer be people who are without food.

from the essay: His Eyes Look Downward and His Heart Looks Upward

In a certain sense, society is a completely abstract concept. A society is not something that exists in isolation; it is made up of units. The first question that arises is, do any number of units, taken together, comprise a society? And if not, what transforms a number of units into one society? Clearly, it is not a question of quantity, but rather one of identity. Taking this idea a step further, in some instances identity is much more important in creating a society than the number of units. This remains true even when small numbers of individual human beings are involved. What transforms a group of people into a nation? Does bringing together one hundred, or a thousand, or a million people make them into a nation? Does randomly placing one letter next to another create a book? Individual units become a society when there are active connections between them. A society can be good or bad, but as long as no interaction exists between units, it is not a society; it is merely a grouping - possibly a very large one - of individual elements.

from the essay: The Individual and Society

The establishment of a society where people can work together and help one another is part of the Jewish way of life. The blueprint for building this kind of society can be found in the Torah. There are specific positive and negative commandments that fall into the general category of *tikkun olam,*" repair of the world.

Every human being is required to work on multiple levels - specific as well as general, material as well as spiritual - to improve human society. The Torah commands us to create things that are useful, and forbids us from destroying anything useful. This is also true of the way we are expected to relate to society. Any anti-social behavior is considered a sin, whether or not it is specifically forbidden in the Torah. A person is required to show even more consideration and respect for another human being than he does for himself. Harm done to another person harms society as a whole. It is an attack on the divine image that exists within every human being.

from the book: The Thirteen Petalled Rose

More than once, the characterization of the Jewish people as "a light among nations" has failed because of the way in which we have tried to achieve this goal. A lighthouse fulfills its function just by being a point of light in the darkness; it does not have to illuminate specific paths. The identity, nature, and mission of the Jewish people should be evident by the way we actually live our lives. They do not have to be announced and publicized. Our existence does not have to be justified by any specific achievement or success; being who we are is sufficient.

from the book: Change and Renewal

Our generation has the potential and ability to make the world a better place. This has also been true of every generation since the first human being became conscious that the world was depraved, polluted, and subjected to evil rulers. Unfortunately, people did not realize that they were in possession of a precious treasure, a key. The key to life had become a key of death because of a pessimistic attitude about this world. People had accepted misery and relentless strife between warring powers as an inevitable part of the human condition.

According to Judaism, the world is inherently good as it stems from the benevolence of our Creator. One of the later biblical prophets expressed the idea in this way: "We all have one father; one God created us all. Why would a brother harm another and break our covenant?" Judaism sees evil as a consequence of human choice, and not as an inexorable part of the world itself. We are commanded by God: "Before you I have laid out life and death, blessing and curse. Choose life." Striving to repair the state of the world is a basic principle of Judaism. From ancient to modern times, the Jewish people, as well as others, have been influenced by and drawn to this idea.

from the essay: To Remake the World into a Kingdom of Heaven

The designation of the Jewish people as "a kingdom of priests and a holy nation" defines us as priests of the world. In the course of our lives, as individuals and as a nation, we must behave as if we are priests whose holy work is to serve the entire world. This definition of the Jewish people does not preclude the possibility that other human beings can also perform holy work and become close to the Divine. But from the moment that the Torah was given to the Jewish people, they were given the responsibility to serve the world as priests. This obligation is not limited to a specific time or place; it holds true at all times and in all places and in all ways in which they live.

from the book: The Thirteen Petalled Rose

It is critical to understand the purpose of the mission. The objective is to bring about the redemption of the world, to prepare for the arrival of the Messiah. As is written in the Passover Haggada, "all of the days of your lives - to bring about the coming of the Messiah." Every day and every night of our lives, we must know that our compliance with commandments and prohibitions, the purpose of everything we do, is to bring about the coming of the Messiah. It is forbidden to be satisfied with anything less.

from the essay: Breathing Life into Elul

Small changes matter. One has to take just one step, or even a half step forward; any motion whatsoever will do as long as there is progress. It might not seem like much, but after years, looking back, a person can say: that was a moment of truth.

Of course, it is also important to dream big dreams - waking dreams, the kind that entail responsibility and spur to action - but small changes matter greatly. The Talmud teaches us that giving charity can be likened to assembling a suit of armor. Just as every scale added to the armor adds to the protection of the entire body, one solitary coin may not have much value, but many coins, saved one at a time, can add up to a considerable sum. When a person decides to tell one less lie every day, or to be a bit more honest in business each day – these minor changes add up; the suit of armor has fewer holes.

One cannot hear a person taking one small step, but when a hundred people take a step together, it makes a big noise. And when a million people take a step forward in unison, it shakes the world. Let us move forward together, with our hearts as one, so we can change the world.

from the essay: On Rosh Hashana

The Exalted & Revered

What makes a person a tzaddik (righteous, holy individual)? The essential question to ask is not "What has he written?" He may have written nothing, yet still be a tzaddik. The question to ask is not "What has he said?" He may have said nothing worth repeating, yet still be a tzaddik. The question to ask is not even "What has he done?" A tzaddik is a tzaddik by essence, by nature; it is what he is. A pearl does not have to do anything; it exists as a pearl. Tzaddikim are not considered to be righteous because of any particular deeds; they are righteous because of who they are. A tzaddik is like a rose, or a star. What does a rose do? What does a star do? They exist, and by sheer existence they are surrounded by a radiance that overflows and has an impact. The radiance of tzaddikim is comprised of the sum total of their deeds, their speech, their smiles, the movements of their hands. Taken all together, this is the essence of a tzaddik.

from the essay: The Righteous

When we celebrate the birthday of a great man, we are essentially acknowledging that, from his very birth, he contributed to the world by the nature of the fact that he was alive. He may not have written books or published anything, but he was known as a person who lived every single day of life to the fullest extent. Others may achieve this for half, or a quarter, or a tenth of their lives, with the remainder of days being lost irretrievably. For a person of greatness, not one day of God-given life is wasted.

from the essay: The Eighteenth of Elul, 5767

According to the Talmud, "if a teacher resembles an angel of God, learn Torah from him; if not, do not." How is one to know what an angel looks like? Who has ever seen an angel of God?

I once heard an answer to this question that resonated as true, even though it was not the clearest answer to this talmudic exhortation. And that is - I may not be able to describe what an angel looks like, but I expect I will know one if I see one standing before me. As with an angel, I can recognize a true teacher of Torah when I see one. Identifying a teacher who can truly transmit the Torah does not depend on specific criteria any more than recognizing an angel depends on wingspan. It depends on my own ability to sense and identify a person of greatness, someone who functions on a plane that is higher than the one in which the usual activity of this world takes place.

from the essay: The Eighteenth of Elul, 5767

People who have achieved a certain level of holiness, like founding fathers of our nation, Abraham, Isaac, Jacob, and Moses, serve as well-known examples for us to try to emulate. But there are also holy people among us who remain completely anonymous, their righteousness unknown.

Like everything holy, the holiness of a person stems from and depends on a connection to the Holy One, blessed be He. Because of this, anyone who has the privilege of making a connection to a holy person is also, in a sense, connecting to the Source of holiness. A holy person is like an angel - a creation that serves as a conduit of holiness from world to world to people. The blessings, actions, prayers, and the very existence of this person enable a flow of holiness to enter our world. One who loves, helps, and clings to a holy person is increasing the scope and the reach of that flow of holiness.

That is why there is a Jewish tradition of cr ating and sustaining deep connections to holy people. Whether holiness stems from greatness in Torah or from an individual's unique personality, it is both a good deed and a commandment to show honor, love, and respect to a holy person as it serves to magnify the potential for holiness in our world.

from the book: The Thirteen Petalled Rose

One of the reasons people read about the lives of great tzaddikim is to learn about the outer capabilities of human spiritual growth. When a person lives among ordinary people, and compares his own growth to that of his neighbors, his frame of reference is limited. If all people in a given land are dwarfs, anyone taller than another by half an inch is considered "tall," even though this is objectively untrue. With regard to spiritual development, it is extremely important for a person to know how much growth is actually humanly possible.

It is easy to feel that you are progressing when you compare yourself to people who are not. It is more difficult when the comparison is to those who are truly great and still growing. People must remember that just as a sapling can reach the height of a giant sequoia, people can strive to be giants. Seeing greatness enables one to realize that more growth remains possible. It is very important to think - "I too can reach great heights; I do not have to stop growing just because I am taller than bushes and grasses."

from the essay: The Way of the Rebbe

It is usually correct to assume that any given individual can have relatively little impact on the larger community. The social environment in which people live usually has a greater impact on people than one individual does.

And yet, in every generation there are some people whose achievements or personalities have an outsize impact that can cause a lasting change in society as a whole. This can occur in a dramatic fashion, as with the decision of a general in a great war, or with a groundbreaking scientific discovery, or with an entirely new approach to matters of the spirit. But it can also occur in a way that is more subtle, as when a person has a unique understanding of the world and, over time, persists in influencing events, be they political, scientific, or artistic, in a way that is consistent with his vision. This influence is based on the individual himself rather than on a single dramatic action or discovery. The words, deeds, and details of the way in which this kind of rare individual lived his life can make a lasting impression on society as a whole. The impact can be great enough to see history as divided into "before" and "after" his life.

from the essay: The Individual and Society in Judaism

When Moses requested of "God of the spirits of all flesh" to identify a person to succeed him as the leader of Israel, God told him to appoint "Joshua the son of Nun, a man of spirit." As a "man of spirit," Joshua had the ability to understand the soul of every individual in the nation. He could reach people in a way that resonated with each one personally. This is a defining quality for a true leader of Israel: a person who can touch each one of six hundred thousand Jewish souls, despite all of their differences. A teacher of Torah is obligated to not only transmit things truly, but also to tailor the message to fit the particular student. He must remain aware of a student's soul, identity, and circumstances, and teach accordingly.

This task is clearly challenging when teaching even two students. When teaching an entire nation, a leader must be able to speak in many "languages" at once, so that all of the people can learn from his words.

from the book: Commentary on the Tanya

The leader is an essential person; a world without a leader is a chaotic world. Even on dry land we need someone to direct us on a path. But when a ship loses her captain, the situation is more dire. A ship in the heart of the sea is not connected to anything stable; there is no way she can arrive at a destination on her own. A captain is needed to navigate continually changing conditions. Without a captain, who will chart the course? Who will decide the direction? Who will understand the patterns of the stars in the sky? Who will see what lies ahead? We are currently like sailors without a captain, on a ship in the middle of the sea.

We are confused and bereft and not on solid ground. What can a person do at a time like this? We know that the course was charted by our captain and that maps were laid out to show the way. Each one of us must keep trying, with every ounce of our ability and strength, to stay the course until we arrive at the end of the journey.

from the essay: The Captain

The Talmud states: "Jacob our father is not dead." As long as the people of Israel, Jacob's descendants, exist in the world, the patriarch Jacob lives on in each and every one. A part of Jacob remains alive in every deed done by a Jew. Similarly, the words of the prayer, "David King of Israel exists and is alive," reminds us that the kingdom of David lives on, even though there is currently no king of Israel. It is not possible to eradicate the House of David from Israel's past or future; we yearn for, and expect its return, every single day.

from the book: My Rebbe

Prologue

from: Creation and Change – In Word and in Deed

Reaching Higher

Page 17
from the essay: Breathing Life into Elul
Page 18
from the essay: The Soul Within Elul
Page 19
from the book: Radiance of the King
Page 20
from the book: My Rebbe
Page 21
from the essay: Breathing Life into Elul
Page 22
from the essay on "Vayetze," 5776
Page 23
from the essay: The New Man
Page 25
from the essay: Thirteenth of Tammuz, 5764

Big Dreams

Page 29
from the book: The Thirteen Petalled Rose
Page 30
from the essay: Human Holiness
Page 31
from the book: The Thirteen Petalled Rose
Page 32
from the book: The Thirteen Petalled Rose
Page 33
from the book: The Soul
Page 34
from the essay: the Eighteenth-of Elul, 5767
Page 35
from the book: The Soul
Page 37
from the book: Change and Renewal

Time

Page 41
from the book: The Thirteen Petalled Rose
Page 42
from the essay: From Childhood to Old Age, Internalizing Education
Page 43
from the essay: Eighteenth of Elul
Page 44-45
from the book: Change and Renewal
Page 46-47
from the book: Radiance of the King
Page 49
from the book: Commentary on the Tanya
Page 50-51
from the essay: The Origin of the Beginning
Page 53
from the essay: On Our Sin of Lost Time

Torah

Page 57
from the essay: The Rebbe, Thirty Years of Leadership
Page 58
from the book: The Thirteen Petalled Rose
Page 59
from the book: The Thirteen

Petalled Rose
Page 60
from the book: The Thirteen-Petalled Rose
Page 61
from the essay: On Learning Torah
Page 62
from the book: Change and Renewal
Page 63
from the book: Change and Renewal
Page 65
from the essay: On Completion of the Torah

Prayer

Page 69
from the essay: Repentance (Teshuva) Preceded Creation of the World
Page 70
from the essay: A Gift from Above
Page 71
from the book: The Thirteen Petalled Rose
Page 72
from the essay: Life in the Present
Page 73
from the essay: Renewal of Prayer
Page 74
from the book: The Thirteen Petalled Rose
Page 75
from the essay: To Pray with Innocence
Page 77
from the essay: To Pray with Innocence

Repentance

Page 81
from the essay: Teshuva, a Return to the Source
Page 82
from the essay: The Cycle of the Year
Page 83
from the essay: Teshuva, a Return to the Source
Page 84
from the essay: Breathing Life into Elul
Page 85
from the essay: Creation and Change – in Word and in Deed
Page 86
from the book: The Thirteen Petalled Rose
Page 87
from the book: The Thirteen Petalled Rose
Page 89
from the essay: Return, Children

Education

Page 93
from the essay: To Repair the World with a Kingdom of Heaven
Page 94-95
from the essay: Curiosity
Page 96
from the essay: Building Character
Page 97
from the essay: The Best Should Teach
Page 98
from the essay: The Best Should Teach
Page 99
from the essay: The Best Should Teach
Page 100-101
from the essay: Jewish Education in the Ancient World
Page 103
from the essay: Good People

Connections

Love for the Jewish People

Freedom & Renewal

Exile & Redempion

Man & the World

The Exalted & Revered

Epilogue